The Building Blocks Of Wealth Creation:

Money Can Change Your Standard Of Living

Dacson Collins

Published by Dacson Collins, 2024.

THE BUILDING BLOCKS OF WEALTH CREATION

Copyright

The publisher has taken all reasonable precautions and accepts responsibility for any errors, deductions, omissions, or damages arising from using the material included herein. It makes adjustments, assisting you in swiftly and effectively reworking and rephrasing your material.

THE BUILDING BLOCKS OF WEALTH CREATION: MONEY CAN CHANGE YOUR STANDARD OF LIVING

Copyright © 2024 Dacson Collins.
Written by Dacson Collins.

THE BUILDING BLOCKS OF WEALTH CREATION

Disclaimer

Every right is reserved. Except as permitted by US copyright law, no portion of this work may be reprinted without the publisher's or author's explicit consent. This book is intended to provide reliable and authoritative information about the topic addressed.

THE BUILDING BLOCKS OF WEALTH CREATION

Book Description

Wealth production is an important topic, and the physical mechanisms of the global market serve as the foundation. People of all ages and races seek riches to improve their quality of life. This intriguing book from Dacson Collins' stables explains how to build wealth and provides proven practical actions to make wealth creation a reality.

Prepare to be informed, transformed in all aspects of life, and properly positioned for money production. This book will enlighten you as you thoroughly examine subjects such as:

• Setting targets

• Leveraging debt

• Funding

• Financing

• Knowing the significant effects of taxes

• Developing a good credit report

This book will guide you toward raising your living level, and you will be a sign of amazement to the world.

THE BUILDING BLOCKS OF WEALTH CREATION

Dedication

I dedicate this book to my immediate family, close friends, and loved ones who inspired me to create and impart the knowledge in it to help others. When our current generation reads this book, it will change them and have a tremendous social impact.

THE BUILDING BLOCKS OF WEALTH CREATION

Table of Contents

Title page

Copyright

Disclaimer

Book Description

Dedication

Chapter 1: | Introduction(Building Blocks of Wealth Creation)

Chapter 2: | Setting targets

Chapter 3: | Leveraging debt

Chapter 4: | Funding

THE BUILDING BLOCKS OF WEALTH CREATION

Chapter 5: | Financing

Chapter 6: | Knowing the Significant effect of taxes

Chapter 7: | Developing a good credit report

Chapter 8: | Conclusion

THE BUILDING BLOCKS OF WEALTH CREATION

Chapter 1

Introduction

Building Blocks of Wealth Creation

It takes time, effort, and discipline to build money. The good news is that everyone can, with the right tactics, accumulate and protect wealth over time. Your chances of success are higher the earlier you begin using these. Setting objectives, leveraging debt, funding, financing, understanding the substantial influence of taxes, and maintaining a favourable credit record are fundamental ideas for accumulating wealth listed below. Let's examine each of these ideas in more detail and see how they might support you in reaching your financial objectives.

THE BUILDING BLOCKS OF WEALTH CREATION

Chapter 2

Setting targets

How are you going to spend your wealth? Do you intend to finance your retirement or perhaps an early one? Cover your children's college expenses? Purchase a second residence? Give your riches to a worthy cause? A crucial first step in accumulating wealth is setting goals. You may make a strategy to assist you in achieving your goals when you have a clear idea of what you want to accomplish.

Establish your financial objectives first. Some examples include debt repayment, house ownership, and retirement savings. Indicate precisely how much money you'll need for each goal and when to complete them.

THE BUILDING BLOCKS OF WEALTH CREATION

After determining your objectives, you must create a strategy for reaching them. You may include setting up a budget to enable you to save more money, advancing your education or career to earn more money, or investing in assets that will increase in value over time. Your strategy must be adaptable, practical, and long-term-oriented. To stay on course, evaluate your progress frequently and make any adjustments.

THE BUILDING BLOCKS OF WEALTH CREATION

Chapter 3

Leveraging debt

As your wealth grows, you'll realise it's sensible to incur debt to fund certain purchases or investments. You can earn points or prizes using your credit card to pay for purchases. You may apply for a mortgage for a primary or secondary house, a home equity loan for home upgrades, or an auto loan to buy a car. Perhaps you'll wish to get a personal loan to start your own business or invest in someone else's.

However, it is critical to manage your debt wisely; taking on too much debt may hamper your progress concerning your wealth-building objectives. To manage debt, keep track of your debt-to-income ratio and ensure that your debt payments fit within your budget. You should also pay off high-interest debt, such as credit card debt, as soon as possible to avoid paying excessive interest costs. Be aware of

THE BUILDING BLOCKS OF WEALTH CREATION

variable or adjustable interest rate products, such as adjustable rate mortgages or balloon payments, because changes in the economy or your circumstances can quickly make those loans.

Indeed, falling into debt can hurt your credit score, and if you fail to pay your debts, you may face personal bankruptcy.

THE BUILDING BLOCKS OF WEALTH CREATION

Chapter 4

Funding

Simply gaining money will not help you accumulate wealth if you squander it all. Furthermore, if you don't have enough money for bills or an emergency, you should put your savings first. Many experts recommend having three to six months' worth of money set aside for such occasions. To place money aside for wealth creation, you can use a budgeting tool or spreadsheet, but a tiny, pocket-sized notepad would also suffice. Record everything you spend, even if it's a small amount; many people are startled to find where all their money goes.

Divide your expenses between needs and wants. Food, housing, and clothing are necessary. Include

THE BUILDING BLOCKS OF WEALTH CREATION

health insurance costs, auto insurance if you own a car, and life insurance if others rely on your income. Many other expenses will be purely optional. Create a savings goal. Once you know how much money you can set aside each month, attempt to stick to it. It does not imply that you must always live frugally. If you're hitting your savings objectives, treat yourself occasionally. You will feel better and more inspired to stay on track. One simple saving option is to set up automatic transfers through your workplace or bank. Please select a specific amount from your pay each month and have it sent to your savings or investing account. Similarly, you can save for retirement by having funds automatically deducted from your pay and deposited into your employer's account. Financial planners typically recommend donating enough to receive your employer's total matching contribution.

Maximise your investment return by searching for savings accounts with the highest interest rates and lowest fees. High-yield savings accounts (HYSAs)

THE BUILDING BLOCKS OF WEALTH CREATION

offer 10 to 12 times the interest rate of a traditional savings account. Certificates of deposit (CDs) can be an effective savings tool if you can afford to store the money for a few months or years. You can only cut so many expenses. If you've already slashed your costs, you should seek ways to increase your income.

THE BUILDING BLOCKS OF WEALTH CREATION

Chapter 5

Financing

Once you've managed to save some money, the next step is to invest it so that it grows. Remember that interest rates on traditional savings accounts are typically relatively low, and your money may lose purchasing value over time due to inflation.

Diversification is perhaps the most crucial investment principle for beginners (or anybody, for that matter). However, it would help if you aim to diversify your investments because investment performance varies over time. Bonds, for example, may provide strong returns if the stock market is in decline.

Investments differ in terms of risk and potential return. Generally speaking, the safer they are, the smaller their prospective return, and vice versa. If

THE BUILDING BLOCKS OF WEALTH CREATION

you're unfamiliar with the various types of investments, it's a good idea to spend some time researching them. While there are other unusual assets, most people prefer to begin with the fundamentals: stocks, bonds, and mutual funds.

Stocks are a corporation's ownership shares. When you acquire stock, you own a small portion of the firm and will benefit from any increase in its share price and dividend payments. Stocks are often regarded as riskier than bonds, but their risk varies significantly from one firm to the next.

Bonds are essentially IOUs issued by a firm or the government. When you purchase a bond, the issuer guarantees to repay your money with interest after a specified period. Bonds are regarded as less risky than equities but with less potential gain. At the same time, certain bonds are more dangerous than others, so you must check the bond rating issued by organisations accordingly.

THE BUILDING BLOCKS OF WEALTH CREATION

Mutual funds are pools of securities, typically stocks, bonds, or a combination. When you buy mutual fund shares, you receive a portion of the pool. Mutual funds' risk levels vary based on the investments they make.

Also, exchange-traded funds (ETFs) are similar to mutual funds in that each share represents a complete portfolio of securities, but ETFs are listed on exchanges and exchanged like stocks. Some ETFs track major stock indexes like the S&P 500, specific industry sectors, or asset classes like bonds and real estate.

THE BUILDING BLOCKS OF WEALTH CREATION

Chapter 6

Knowing the Significant effect of taxes

Taxes are a frequently ignored impediment to your wealth-building efforts. Of course, we all pay income and sales taxes when we earn and spend money, but our investments and assets may also be taxed. That's why it's critical to understand your tax liabilities and devise measures to mitigate their impact.

Investing in tax-advantaged accounts is a simple approach to reducing your tax burden. These accounts, such as 529 college savings programmes, individual retirement accounts (IRAs), and 401(k) plans, provide tax breaks to help you save money and lower your tax liability. Contributions to a typical IRA or 401(k), for example, are tax-deductible, which means you can reduce your taxable income and save money on taxes in the year

THE BUILDING BLOCKS OF WEALTH CREATION

you make them. They also grow tax-deferred, which means that when you retire, the impact will be minor, and you will be at a lower tax rate. Investment gains in a Roth IRA or Roth 401(k) are tax-free, which means that you can grow and withdraw funds from a Roth account without paying taxes on any of the income or profits.

Another option for reducing taxes is to consider the timing and location of your assets. Holding investments for more than a year allows you to benefit from the reduced long-term capital gains tax rate, which is typically lower than the short-term capital gains and income tax rates.

Also, keep in mind where specific assets are stored. If given the option, an income-producing asset such as a dividend-paying stock or corporate bond should be held in a tax-advantaged account such as a Roth IRA, where payments will not result in taxable events. A growth stock that will solely provide capital gains (rather than income) may be better off in a taxable account.

THE BUILDING BLOCKS OF WEALTH CREATION

Chapter 7

Developing a good credit report

Building and maintaining a solid credit score is a crucial step toward long-term wealth growth and preservation. If you have an excellent credit history and a high credit score, you will be able to get a reduced interest rate and better loan terms, potentially saving you hundreds of dollars in interest payments over time. You can maintain a decent credit score by following a few essential measures.

Payment history is one of the most critical elements affecting your credit score. To keep a decent credit score, you must always pay your payments on time. Late payments, even those made a few days late, can significantly negatively influence your credit score.

THE BUILDING BLOCKS OF WEALTH CREATION

Another significant aspect influencing your credit score is your credit usage or the amount of credit you use compared to the amount you have available. To maintain a decent credit score, reduce your credit utilisation to less than 30% of your available credit. It is recommended that you check your credit report frequently to ensure that all of the information is correct and up-to-date. Today, multiple firms offer free credit reports. Errors on your credit report might lower your credit score, so challenge any inaccuracies you discover.

Every credit application can have a modest negative impact on your credit score. To keep a decent credit score, avoid creating too many new accounts hastily. However, if you do not use credit cards or do not have enough credit lines open, you may suffer from a lack of credit history. So, open some credit cards and get some loans, but don't overdo it. By following these methods and developing solid credit habits, you may improve your credit score and increase your borrowing power in the long run.

Chapter 8

Conclusion

Even though methods to become wealthy quickly occasionally may seem alluring, the most reliable method of accumulating wealth is by consistently saving and investing, then watching your money increase over time. Starting small is acceptable. The most crucial thing is to get started as soon as possible. Make money, save it, and make wise investments with it. Reduce your tax liability and safeguard your valuables with insurance. Remember that accumulating wealth is a process rather than a final goal. Enjoy your victories along the way and resist the need to give up in the face of difficulties or setbacks. You can attain financial success and accumulate riches over time with perseverance, self-control, and a clear understanding of your objectives.

THE BUILDING BLOCKS OF WEALTH CREATION

www.ingramcontent.com/pod-product-compliance
Lightning Source LLC
Chambersburg PA
CBHW072058230526
45479CB00010B/1137